SURVIVAL BARTERING

Duncan Long

Loompanics Unlimited Port Townsend, WA

SURVIVAL BARTERING

Printed in USA

Published by:
Loompanics Unlimited
PO Box 1197
Port Townsend, WA 98368

ISBN 0-915179-37-7
Library of Congress Catalog Card Number 86-080537

To Maggie

TABLE OF CONTENTS

INTRODUCTION

I am hoping that you'll never need to know much about what's in this book; but you might need it very badly if you ever need it. You might need to know how to barter just to survive. Apparently, you've been watching the evening news, too. You see the problems that may go away or may develop into a real disaster for all of us.

If, for some reason, our money system of economy ever goes out of existence, you many need to barter to keep your family and your business operating. As you'll see, barter isn't all that hard and we use many of its elements in our everyday existence.

You do need to plan ahead and be ready to act if and when the economy of your area — or of your world — comes to an end and barter takes its place. You can't just read this book. You must read it and then act and practice.

Also, it is important that you can be in an area where barter can act unhindered and where the people can create a community which can police and support itself. If your area needs utilities and trucked-in supplies to support its population, then an economic collapse might degenerate into year-round riots where no one could create, manufacture, or supply the needs of your community.

What would happen if someone shut off the utilities in your area and quarantined it? Could the people work together or would it be every man for himself with the strongest stealing from the others? Your first move for surviving may be to leave the area you're in for one where you can work and barter to survive.

Learning how to barter will be like an insurance policy: hopefully you'll never need it, but if you do, it's great to have made the effort and sacrifices to get it.

Good luck.

BARTER AND MONEY

Many of us are unaware of the bartering that is going on about us everyday. Barter goes on with — or without — your awareness. Chances are, it's alive and well in your neighborhood.

Big business and many professionals barter goods and services almost excessively while the tax man gnashes his teeth. Black markets and truck stores also barter to the tune of the same grinding.

Some barter to beat taxes, some to live in a better style, and some just for the fun of it.

Barter is almost second nature to people. It allows for specialization in society and has encouraged mankind to set up villages and cities where barterers can more easily carry on their trades.

In these days of all too possible economic collapse, war scares, and disaster nightmares, barter could easily become a necessity for each of us. If and when banks take an endless holiday and your government's money becomes completely worthless and unacceptable to anyone, you and your friends can still carry out your transactions through barter. Barter could allow you and your community to continue to function. Areas not able to switch to barter would quickly sink into chaos or anarchy. Given time, such an area would sink into its own localized dark ages.

Many books have been written about barter. Most tend to view it as an anachronism which man has outgrown. These writers explore barter as an interesting hobby which may also turn a profit but not as a way of supporting a family or running a business. They see barter mostly only for the rare individual who wants to play with a new hobby.

Perhaps.

But perhaps barter will become a necessity. Perhaps it isn't really a rare form of trade but something we use every day.

Imagine for a moment that barter never really stopped but has rather been stylized to speed up trade. We have not really quit bartering but have rather changed the process into the "money" idea.

No, I don't think that's a mental-gymnastic trick. Don't we all barter our time, goods, and services for money? Didn't money once represent (if in fact it wasn't) silver and gold? Isn't money a sort of three-way barter with your government playing middleman and taxing the whole system for the government's sometimes dubious services — including coinage?

If you can view our money system as a type of barter, many barter concepts can be quickly carried over from your everyday money experiences.

Just what is money? We take it for granted.

Money must come in small, easily portable, known units of (ideally) fairly constant value. It must be readily available and must be easy to exchange for what you need (provided the price is right and you have enough money to barter with).

The point is: many of our good shopping habits are also good bartering habits. Society would not have as much trouble switching to barter as one might think, at least on the individual level (electronic banking and multi-national corporations would be a different story). Don't think of barter as something exotic or foreign. Using money is a form of barter. When money falters, we can switch to another barter system or items. For a culture to continue to exist, such a switch would be practical as well as possible.

When money starts to wander away from its ideal form of units with constant value which are small and easily portable, people use some other item to replace the government's money. In the past, run-away inflation, depression, or governmental instability all have caused barterers to bring out their own coinage: soap, bullets , silver or gold coins, cigarettes, candy, or you-name-it. Just so long as it has the qualities of being small and of a constant, known value and is readily available in a quantity to support trade, it can be used for barter "money."

Supply and demand works for all barter items (including money). The more there is, the less it's worth; if it becomes scarce, its value goes up. (If it becomes too scarce, value may be hard to establish and it may become hard to exchange items for something else. People may also learn to make-do with something else.)

If you've never really depended on barter, it's not too hard to imagine a time when it might be an absolute necessity. Even in your everyday life.

Imagine driving along on a vacation. Your car breaks down and you have lost your I.D., checks, cash, and credit cards. Suddenly you're in the barter system, like it or not.

That peanut butter sandwich you wrinkled your nose at earlier suddenly becomes the only meal you can afford. Or does it? You barter your dishwashing talents at a restaurant for some free meals.

You barter your old gold class ring (that your spouse doesn't like too well anyway) with the local antique/coin/whatever dealer on a side street. Now you have cash.

But not enough for car repairs... Well, you could get someone to wire money or whatever but... by throwing in your snow tires (which have been taking up room in your trunk since last spring), your watch, *and* the money from your old class ring, your car is repaired and you're on your way.

Farfetched? Well, yes, probably. You can imagine it, though, and it does happen every day to people who keep their wits when they get into tight spots during their normally uneventful days.

Certainly not farfetched if the economy is in trouble or the government's currency has become worthless overnight and the village you're stranded in isn't that crazy about the cash you have.

Knowing how to barter may sometimes make things quite a bit easier for you. It might even save your life. History is full of times when people fled their countries carrying barter items to make their escape possible. It has happened; it could happen again.

Barter can give you the edge you need to survive.

BARTER AND SELF-RELIANCE

Back in the dark ages, during my senior year of college, I had a rather strange experience (as college experiences go). A snow storm sprang up suddenly on the Kansas plains and several hours later the area was brought to a halt by the storm. This much snow was rare in Kansas and took everyone by surprise, including road crews and the weather man.

I was an off-campus student and had been commuting to class. I was without bed and board at the college when the blizzard stranded me at the college. Suddenly, things which I had in my pockets and car were all I owned.

I had to become a beggar to obtain room and food for the remainder of the day and night. Fortunately, my father was in the area and rescued me. The roads weren't as bad as I thought and he was able to drive well in the snow and knew which roads in the area were cleared.

Nothing was hurt other than my pride (begging doesn't build the ego — though perhaps the soul). This did wake me up. This was when I realized that some day, if money suddenly became worthless, traffic ground to a stop from lack of gasoline, a nation-wide strike occurred, or a war took place, most of us would be hurting very quickly for what would be considered necessities in our everyday life.

Out of the experience was born two goals: That I would try to be as prepared for the unexpected as possible and be as self-sufficient as possible (no matter when or where) and that I would be aware of how to obtain what I needed by trade and improvisation, without lowering my moral standards because of the new circumstances.

Pre-war Germany and WWII events give many examples of what could happen in a modern society suddenly plunged into problems. Though there is not sufficient room to cover specifics, this period shows what can happen to a prosperous country and how quickly it can be forced to change habits and methods of business when the government's money and policies fail the people.

When money becomes worthless or hard to come by then something else will become the new "money." American G.I.'s discovered a wide variety of barter currency: chocolate, stockings, coffee, tobacco, and sugar. Although such items had intrinsic worth, they were often not used (just as you don't melt down your pennies for copper wiring but rather trade them for the finished product). These items were traded back and forth like a real type of coinage. Cigarettes, for example, were traded and accepted by smokers and non-smokers alike.

During times when barter currency is created, anyone capable of creating the barter product is in the position of being able to be a "mint" and strike his own "coins." Just as the government is able to increase its wealth by making money with a higher face value than the materials and energy needed to create the money, so, too, can a manufacturer "make money," making barter money. After paying for materials, labor, etc., he'll still have some barter "value" left over. He has created extra wealth.

If you find yourself in such a position, there are some things to guard against. First, you must be sure you produce a product equal to, or better than, other similar currency being used. Second, you must be sure you don't flood the market with too much barter currency. The first is tantamount to counterfeiting, the second would cause inflation of the new "currency." You would have the same headaches governments do when they print up their monies. Take heart. You can't do any worse than many of them have!

Barter currency will probably be temporary or change to a different form periodically. Don't try to save it up or spend too much on machinery to create it.

The currency may change, a new government may spring up to outlaw the barter currency and replace it with its own coinage, or the barter currency may be replaced by direct barter where people trade directly for what they need without using any intermediate barter currency. Possibly all three forms will co-exist.

During the troubled depression times in the U.S. of the 1930's, barter was quite common on a one-to-one basis. Farm animals were traded for implements (after a little haggling); preachers were paid with eggs, butter, cream and milk; mills traded ground flour and its by-products for labor and wheat (and made profits from the difference between what was traded for and what was brought in).

The 30's (and 20's) also produced the traveling salesman (and numerous jokes and stories about their profession) for companies like Raleigh, Watkins Products, and later McNess Products. These salesmen traveled by buggy and Model T Fords peddling their products: extracts, pie fillings, shredded coconut, spices and flavorings along with fly sprays, salves, liniments, and soaps — to name only a few of their products.

The coming of the salesman was a big event for many, especially in the Midwest where the population was principally rural. He was invited to stay for meals or even overnight while he entertained with news from the surrounding communities. The salesman would take good ol' money for goods, of course, but eggs, chickens, and butter were also exchanged for products, as well as meals and lodging. Even when customers paid in cash, lodging and meals sometimes had to be "thrown-in" so the salesman could have a place to stay and something to eat.

Many salesmen were flamboyant and successful. Some had trouble with "stretching the truth" about their products. Some told or promised almost anything to make a sale and never fulfilled their bargains after they'd received their end of payment. Remember *The Music Man*? All too real.

On the local level much trade took place in rural areas during the 30's as well. Newspaper subscriptions or life insurance policies were often traded for gasoline, chickens or the like. One old movie theatre bill shows the general idea in prices and trades. Tickets were 10¢ and 25¢ each. The movie theatre also accepted in trade: eggs @ 15¢ a dozen; yellow corn, 30¢ a bushel; white corn, 27¢ per bushel; wheat, 50¢ per bushel. Can you imagine standing in line while you carried payment for your wife and six kids? Worse yet, how would you like to work selling tickets!?!

This same period also saw barter agreements between governments and those who could work but hadn't a job. Road crews were formed from those who exchanged hard labor for tax payments.

(Labor is like a commodity; it can be traded for other "items," money (our normal procedure now), or other types of labor. Think too, how much easier it is to trade in some products than others. In the above movie theatre, how much better to have eggs to trade rather than bushels of wheat.)

Any time of war, economic problems, government instability, emergency, or social unrest can create a time when money becomes worthless and barter takes over.

Governments sometimes have emergency money printed to replace their old currency which becomes worthless during an emergency. Needless to say this puts extra money into the pockets of the government and allows them to buy and sell and decide who else will do the same *if* people accept the new currency. Usually the new money isn't accepted with open arms, so the government may pass laws which "encourage" everyone to use the money.

So, black markets and dealing under the table will be the general rule when the government forces money on the public.

If you ever find yourself with emergency currency, be sure to spend it quickly (not recklessly — there's a difference) when you find what you need and try barter in a gift form to put grease on the squeaky business of using governmental money. All sorts of items may slide into sight when barter grease is generously used. Straight barter may also cause store keepers to "remember" items stored under the counter when you're "out of money but willing to trade."

Whatever you do, don't save a government's emergency currency as its value may fall very quickly if things get worse... just when you need money to spend.

Barter can help you get around other problems, too. Price controls, currency shortage, unfair taxes, or bad regulations can all be short-circuited by skillful use of bartering. Just don't be too trusting or too blatant.

Many of those who barter over a long time feel that barter tends to bring the value of items into focus. Unlike checks and credit cards, barter really tells you what something is worth to you in a concrete, straightforward way.

Barter also often makes storing up excessive wealth seem — excessive. Just as a hundred dollars in the form of 100 silver dollars seems larger than one 100 dollar bill, so bartering commodity for commodity without the symbolism of money representation shows you in a three-dimensional way just how much you have. Now your heart knows how much wealth you have instead of just your head (and maybe your accountant).

For many, richness of life means money in the bank or money squirreled away somewhere. This is fine if not carried out excessively. We've all heard about the rich guy living in rags, freezing to death while he has lots of money in the bank, walls of his house, mattress, jars, and assorted piggy banks. Is that richness of life?

Surely being wealthy has (or should have) something to do with the quality of life and whether it allows you to pursue the interests you have. Richness doesn't have to be and shouldn't be the amount or number of items you have but rather the standard of living you have.

Our current technology allows us to do and enjoy things which were unavailable to kings in years past. Surely a king in the Middle Ages sitting in a smoke-filled, drafty castle, smelling unwashed bodies and squinting into the darkness never dreamed of the wealth each of us takes for granted. Living in the standard of yesterday's kings would make you today's pauper — with a little superstition thrown in.

During a time of a serious crisis, when barter becomes a necessity for survival, the more self-sufficient you are, the better trades you can make. If a good deal isn't available, you can wait until one comes along. If you can barter when it suits you, you will be able to take advantage of good deals, come out ahead in the long run, and gradually increase your wealth. Now is the time to start getting the materials and knowledge to become as self-sufficient as possible. Learn to do things and how to make things which are needed by your family. Obtain the tools, machinery, skills, and books, now.

A home which can supply its own utility needs is also essential. This means you should check into heating, sewage disposal, water supplies, and maybe even a way of supplying mechanical or electrical power for your tools and your electrical standard of living which you've grown accustomed to. Try to figure out what's essential and what can be done away with.

When preparing to become self-sufficient, try to decide what is a necessity and what is a luxury. Then make a priorities list. Start at the top and work down whenever possible.

Stewardship should be practiced by you and your family. A family whose members are careful and thoughtful can live at a very high standard for a very long time. A rambunctious group can waste their advantages, destroy their assets through rough abuse, and be paupers in a short time.

Careful, thoughtful use of your assets may not guarantee wealth, but wasteful use will guarantee poverty. Be sure your younger family members understand this, too. Their cooperation could be essential if times really become bad quickly.

Skillful use of barter can make it possible to increase your wealth. Therefore you should always be alert during barter bargaining and careful; a few large mistakes will undo a lot of care.

In conjunction with barter, your standard of living can be maintained, or even raised, if you learn to recycle, repair, substitute, and do without.

Recycling is something that manufacturers do and are lauded for while the common man is made to feel like a skinflint if he does any recycling. Learn to buck the social pressure and use second-hand items. When a tool or appliance is ruined beyond repair, cannibalize the parts for other machinery. Sometimes having the right used part saves a lot of time and resources spent looking for a new part that isn't any better than a used one. Be sure you don't get carried away with recycling; when something is nothing more than junk, get rid of it.

Repairing is similar to recycling. Manufacturers have encouraged us to throw away and buy new. Repairing anything is often cheaper than trading for a new item.

Substitution can also save a lot of resources. Also, look for items capable of serving several functions. Some tools are capable of doing only one thing while others are tailored to do several tasks.

Doing without often saves a lot of time and resources. Not satisfying every whim also seems (or maybe even *is*) morally uplifting. Judging from the problems of the "idle rich" this may really be so. In any event, not getting every little thing which strikes your fancy saves a lot of resources for your other needs. Give some time and thought to what your needs really are. Doing without — even if only for a while — can give some time for weighing your real needs and for avoiding obtaining something on an impulse.

When possible try to get the simplest tools and ways of doing things. Simple machines are often less apt to fail than complex machines. Also, try to get machinery that has stood the test of time. In-field tests often bring out problems the manufacturer never dreamed of.

Unfortunately many "creators" do their field-testing via consumers and complaints about products. Just don't be too afraid of new, better ways either, if they really seem to be what they claim to be.

Time may not be money, but it can be wealth. Try to keep your time uncluttered and as simple as possible. Have time to think out problems. Time to think can give you an edge over those who jump into jobs, then spend their time undoing things before they can start trying the right way. There is almost always a better way to do something.

Thinking is also a good practice before entering into any bartering agreement. A little thinking can prevent a lot of mistakes and save a lot of endless waste and frustration. When in doubt, think.

TYPES OF BARTER

There a number of types of barter. They are often combined and can be overly complex so that it is hard to analyze just exactly what type is being used or not, but knowing what is going on may help you somewhat. You should be aware of the different types of barter and be sure you are not missing out on one of the types. If you limit yourself to just a few styles, you'll be losing out on quite a bit of opportunity and chances for gain.

The simplest form of barter is the gift exchange. This may be an exchange of actual gifts or may be of information or favors. The return gift may follow the first immediately or may come days, months, or years later. In such a case the receiver of the first gift would "owe one" to the second. Though gifts are given so that it appears they are not a trade or barter, anyone who treats them other than a trade will be considered to be rude or selfish. The true gift, without strings, is rare.

Gifts need not be of the same type but should be of the same value or, in the case of a group of items given for one gift, of the same total value. Thus a physical item may be given for information or the like as long as both parties feel that the gifts are of equal value. If the receiver of the first gift does not have a countergift to give in the near future, he should be sure to acknowledge that he owes a favor to the gift giver.

The only exception to the exchange of gifts is the community gift giving which takes place when officials leave office, a marriage takes place, etc., when a return gift is not expected. The person *is* expected to give gifts to the next person who is the object of the community's gift giving, however, so that all things even out — more or less — in the long run.

The second form of barter is the one-to-one trade between individuals. Unlike the gift exchange, the two barterers can haggle on the terms of the trade and can decide not to trade if they wish. Most trades may be of physical objects, but ideas, information, services, and skills can all be bartered. Any of these groups of items can be exchanged for any of the others so that it wouldn't be rare to see an object traded for information or service.

The third form of barter can take many convoluted twists so that it is hard to actually see what all is going on. In its simplest form a go-between makes a trade for two parties. He knows that one has something the other needs and vice versa so he carries out the bargaining and the trade himself, working with each of the other two. In reality, this form of barter often includes four or five trades with the middle man going to four or five people to make separate trades until he gets all the proper items lined up for the final trade for what he wants.

Money is a sort of the third form of barter. The government becomes the middleman to enable you to trade your work time for items you need. Third-form barter saves time for the people on either end of the barter while the middle man often spends more time creating the trade (though not always as in the case of the government's money which is produced quite quickly through automated processes). In exchange for the extra work the middleman does in setting up the trade, he extracts his price in goods, information, etc., from the people on either side of the barter deal to pay for all his efforts and foot work. (Inflation and taxes are two of the prices users of money often pay in the case of their government performing the third form of barter with its money.)

When a government's money quits being accepted for the third form of barter, another form of barter currency often fills the vacuum left by the money. The person who can create such barter currency becomes the new middleman of the third-form barter and can enjoy the benefits of extracting his pay automatically (just as the government did) if he can produce his barter money at a lower "cost" in supplies and labor than the "money" is worth. The difference between its value and the cost to produce it is the middleman's profit for his service of creating the new barter currency.

Though most trading is straight value barter with the value of the item being traded worth as much as the item traded for, the traditional "horse trader" is the person who seeks to actively increase his "profits" by coming out ahead on each trade. Such a person must be very alert and take advantage of specific needs that some individuals have and then trade around to meet the needs, keeping a little extra for his efforts. A horse trader must be shrewd, profit-oriented, and often is perceived as not completely aboveboard in all of his dealings. When trying to trade to increase your profits, it's probably best to avoid all appearances of being a horse trader; rather appear to be a regular guy who just manages to come out ahead from time to time.

If the money system breaks down and the local community is completely disrupted by a nation-wide war or other disaster, you may have to get together with others to create a barter economy. This won't just happen (or at least not quickly enough to do many of the community members any good) so it must be encouraged and helped along.

First of all, enough people must be brought together to supply goods and services for all the basic needs of the majority of the community's members. This allows for some specialization and more efficient production of goods as the same machinery and tools won't be duplicated by various members of the community if one person can do a job and share — through barter — with others. This creates a savings of machinery — and often time and raw materials as well — since the person doing the work becomes more efficient at it with time and practice. This savings is then passed along to the community members and the general wealth and standard of the community group increases.

An area where everyone can gather in safety to carry on their bartering is also needed: a community marketplace. If law enforcement officials are not available, barterers will have to arm themselves or "hire" protectors by trading for the services of capable individuals to protect merchants and their customers and to keep things under control. A central location to all members of the community is best for the marketplace with a time set for engaging in barter. By setting aside a certain time for the bartering to take place, workers and craftsmen are able to spend much of their time working to produce their product, using only the time set aside for the actual bargaining. This savings of work time will also help the community by increasing the worker's output as less of his time is wasted waiting on solitary barterers.

The community must foster a feeling of obligation toward the common good. The less government — other than volunteer work — the better, as it will prevent the taxation of workers and the lowering of the output/wealth of your barter community. An old established economic system can stand a lot of taxation; a little taxation will kill a new, small economic system.

If possible, encourage some specialization and interdependence between the members of your barter community so that common needs are met and products and services are complimentary to each other. Whenever you can, engage in barter that is of the equal value swap and those who are horse traders at heart should be discouraged from practicing their first love.

If some type of barter money is developed (eggs, ammunition, etc.), try to get a standard established so that inferior products don't create an "inflation" during which those who save goods lose out to those who spend barter money wildly and recklessly.

In a barter community, everyone can become wealthy (i.e. have a high standard of living) at the same time. If everyone produces more than they need, the excess can be traded for other goods, provided everyone is not duplicating someone else's product. Thus, if your community diversifies in what each person is producing, you can all grow wealthy together. Because this is completely the opposite of the common dog-eat-dog system where everyone producing the same goods and surpluses lowers everyone's profit, the community will tend to encourage enterprise and hard work. Though you wouldn't want to regulate what people produce (competition — or the threat of it — encourages lower barter prices), people should be urged to diversify in what they produce to promote the wealth of the barter community's individuals. Utopia? No, but hardly a retreat to the dark ages either.

If and when cheaters are encountered in the barter

market, you must spread the word in your barter community. Cheaters lessen the wealth of those who are cheated and, little by little, hurt everyone in the community.

If your area is open to traders from outside your community, then everyone should be on the lookout for those who are not above-board in their dealings. Such people will be carrying wealth out of your community group and leaving little or nothing behind. Several crooked "horse traders" passing through your community can quickly bleed it of much of its wealth and set it back months and even years in its economic growth.

HOW TO GET GOOD DEALS BY BARTERING

"Barter" doesn't mean "free." People who are used to paying cash often feel that trading for something without spending cash means it is free. Not so. Whatever you traded has value. That's the cost of what you bartered for.

Likewise, once you've spent your barter wealth, you've used all your spending power. When you're short of things to barter, you're just as bankrupt as the man who's run out of cash.

In everyday life nothing's free. That's true of loans (and gifts as we've seen). When you borrow something, you're engaging in a small barter. In effect, you're promising to let the loaner borrow something from you in the future or to give him something or a favor in return. You "owe him one."

When you borrow something, remember that you are in effect going into debt with that person. A good type of "interest" to pay for the loan is to return the borrowed item in better shape than before you borrowed it. If this isn't possible, then a small gift — in addition to the "owe him one" in the future — might be in order. Care and thought is required in not making your friend your newest enemy. Shakespeare's "Neither a borrower nor a lender be" is not such bad advice most often.

Barter business is like being a salesman. Sometimes you can't just wait until business comes to you; you must stir things up and scare up some business. The world does *not* seek the inventor of the mousetrap unless he lets everyone know about his new invention. Sometimes it pays to "advertise." Let people know what you have and that you are interested in bartering.

If you have succeeded in becoming somewhat self-sufficient, you may find that you are too productive from time to time. You may produce more than you need. This isn't bad if you can barter your surplus products for other needs. Sometimes — let's imagine — your garden may produce lots of tomatoes while the squirrels capture your pecans. This is when you barter your extra tomatoes for your neighbor's pecans. Trade excess for someone else's excess when possible for best bargains. If trade is impossible, learn how to store food by canning and other processes.

One form of barter is the gift exchange. For some reason, our culture demands that the gift exchange must appear to be gifts exchanged with no strings attached. A quick or poorly done exchange brands someone as crass while a forgotten repayment of the gift — or a gift that isn't as valuable as the first — is an insult. Care must be taken!

Usually, the gift exchange is forgotten about in business until a friendship of sorts is struck up between the businessmen or the businessman and his customers. A gift is often used to break the ice or set a favorable stage for some request. (Bribes are illegal gift exchanges.)

After the first gift is given, the receiver "owes one" to the giver. This allows him to make his gift, and the first trade has been carried out. For some reason this really breaks the ice sometimes and makes it possible for the trading of information, items, and you-name-it without the embarrassment which would occur without the preliminary gift exchange.

Always have a "reason," however flimsy, for giving the gift and don't belittle the gift you give or receive. At the same time, when you give a gift, you must make it seem like "no big deal." Care must be given to choose the suitable gift, time its giving, and react to receiving the countergift. Once all the preliminary moves are over, the stage is set for bigger exchanges. You can skip the gift exchange, but it can really be used to put everyone at ease for major bartering if it is used properly.

Don't waste too much time on little trades or preliminary trades or gift exchanges. Just as a merchant will go broke if he spends his time selling only cheap items which give little profit on each sale, so you will go broke if you spend as much time haggling on small trades as you do on large ones. The smaller the trade item's worth, the less time you should spend in bartering it.

When bartering for life or death items like medication, reloaded ammunition or guns, or electrical/heating items and work, be extra careful to be sure the person is giving you something which is what it's supposed to be and which will work properly. Any malfunction with some items can be fatal to the user. If you have any doubts or the trade seems too good to be true, don't gamble with your safety or health. You must know about the item or be capable of checking it out. Don't trade for doubtful items your life or health may depend upon.

It also pays to know about items whose value may change from time to time or even day to day. Demand can change an item's value and if you trade for what something was worth a week ago to a shrewd bargainer, you may find that you've lost quite a bit when the item's value fell earlier. If you can't keep up on something's value, then check with several people that are dealing in the same item. Shop for the "best price." Taking a little time and checking things out can save a lot of heartache when making large trades.

The best barter deals can occur when someone has too much or when their business or trade is doing poorly. This is when they will make good deals to keep things going rather than going out of business. Don't take so much advantage of such people that you have a guilty conscience, but at the same time, you will be helping them stay in business and should not feel guilty about taking advantage of their good barter deals.

Along the same lines, some of the best barter deals can be obtained when things are seasonal, and are currently out of season. Winter coats — for example — are always cheapest in the summer. If you can plan ahead by about a half a year and have enough surplus goods to trade, you can really take advantage of seasonal items and get the absolute best deals by trading when they are out of season with your goods that are in season or non-seasonal.

Sometimes, bartering with those who are pretty well supplied is easier or at least less traumatic, than with the "poor." Those who can trade on a take-it-or-leave-it basis are less pushy and worry less about getting a bad deal. Seek out those who will bargain without high pressure and who don't drag out the trade to be sure-beyond-a-doubt that you've given them the absolutely best deal. The time and aggravation you save yourself will be worth it many times over.

When you invest in items to barter, don't put all your eggs in one basket. Do things like the wealthy investors do: diversify. If you specialize, you may be able to corner the market, but you may also find that the items you have a monopoly on suddenly are replaced by a cheaper item or the public has found they can do without what you are bartering. Water and air are about the only things that people cannot do without and even if you had the sources of those pretty well covered, someone would probably find a new source of both.

Try to spread yourself out and have different commodities to trade and several different skills to offer to others. When things break down and barter becomes your livelihood, it would never hurt to be too talented. A Renaissance man need never go hungry if he keeps his wits about him and his skills polished.

The first time you trade with someone, give them a really good bargain on their trade. This will make them feel good and therefore they'll want to trade with you again and it will give you a good reputation as word of mouth advertises your good deals. A satisfied "customer" has always been a good way to stay in business without having to leave town in front of an angry mob. Good deals mean more deals.

Get to know the people you're dealing with. Being friendly and taking time to be courteous will improve your trades, make people feel like giving you a good deal and may even keep you from getting ulcers. If bartering with you is a pleasant experience, then people will not mind doing it again and may even seek you out. If you make a trade in a time of trauma and treat people as if they are trying to cheat you, you may get a good deal one time, but you probably won't get many more from that person or his friends. The only thing to be careful of is that you become too friendly to the point that you can't say no to a poor deal without offending your "friend" in trade. Don't let people use this against you. Be friendly but firm. Be able to give a friendly "no."

Don't get too anxious to make a large trade. The person you are dealing with — especially if it is the first time and they don't know you too well — is apt to think you're trying to trick him into making a mistake in trading with you. Take your time and help the person to see that they are getting a good deal from you. It might not hurt to have some mutual acquaintances or some other people you've traded with as "references" for the really unsure person you may be trading with. Sometimes just mentioning a few names will reassure the person you're dealing with without actually having anyone contacted at the time of the trade.

In a barter economy, the government won't be there to protect the public from smaller (and perhaps even larger) frauds. Let the buyer (trader) beware. This means that you must take a little time to inspect the object you're trading for and know whether or not it's what you want and what kind of shape it's in. When you get home and your new prize comes apart in your hands, it's probably too late to bargain for a better deal. You must inspect things carefully and bargain from your knowledge during the trade.

Don't be afraid to point out faults, but do so in a diplomatic way. If you make the person feel like a cheat, then he probably won't trade with you again and may not finish the deal. A little tact and wisdom will enable you to get a better trade by pointing out an item's faults — or apparent faults — while still maintaining a happy atmosphere for everyone engaged in the trade.

Some things to think about: are there any obvious faults, imperfections, or breaks; does it operate properly; how old is it; is it worn; how hard is it to find replacement parts or repair it; does it look tarnished or worn; will it be hard to move or cause you inconvenience when you receive it? All or any of these can give you a trading edge if pointed out tactfully. Some barterers like to work as a team with two people. One is the person who points out faults in the trader's item and the other looks at the good points of the object. Good guy/bad guy teamwork in action. This may work once or twice but people soon catch on. It might be worth trying if you have one special deal you're bargaining for. It can also backfire with some introverted people who dislike a "crowd" and may be irritated by someone who is making their deal go sour by pointing out faults. Be sure your team can play the parts correctly before you try this out.

Ask questions and don't volunteer too much information about what you have to trade. Try to find an object's shortcomings yourself and ask a few questions about it after you've inspected it. Try to ask questions that make it sound like you know what you're doing. This will encourage the other trader to be honest and will prevent him from thinking he may get an extra good deal from someone who doesn't know what they're doing. Don't mislead someone by not telling them something important about what you have to trade (like the fact that the thing doesn't work at all) but don't go out of your way to point out obvious minor faults in the object you're trading away — the person you're dealing with may not be concerned about the faults, but may use it for trade leverage if they think you think it's important.

If something doesn't work or doesn't work properly then it is traded "as is." This means that both parties realize that the piece may well be a pile of junk but can probably be repaired — by someone who knows what he's doing. Don't expect more than what you see when something is sold "as is." If it were in perfect running order, the person would say so to get a better deal.

When the other trader asks questions about your goods, don't hesitate to answer his questions but don't tell too much or stretch out the trade too much by volunteering more information than either of you really wants to hear. Of course with some objects, you may need to tell a little to point out its good points and tell of its history. There is a difference between selling a product and answering questions. Don't be shy to point out all of the good points of your trade offering if the other barterer seems to be taking some of its finer points for granted or misses the greatness of what you're offering!

On large items like pieces of machinery, produce, or farm animals, you may offer to move the object or deliver it as part of the barter whether you're bartering the object away or trading for the item to be moved. Don't be afraid to bring other such points into the trade or point out the moving problems involved, to get a better trade for yourself.

Whenever possible, let the other guy set the "price" of your trade first. Often, he'll give you a better deal than you expected. The trick is not to show your surprise at the good offer he makes. If you're dealing with a seasoned trader who doesn't make a first offer, then you should try to make an offer that is a lot better — for you — than you expect to get. Just don't make it too unreasonable (though people have done this and been flabbergasted when the other person agreed to the deal without hesitation). Try to keep a poker face and try for the best deal you can get at the onset.

The usual practice is to dicker over the deal after each side makes his own offer. If one of you is using some sort of barter money, then the seller will ask for a price higher than the buyer (the one with the barter money) expects to pay and the buyer will make an offer considerably lower than he expects to finally pay.

One or the other of you may wish to make a quick deal or lay the groundwork for future trades by accepting at this point. If so, the trade is over and should be finalized as soon as possible. A real taboo is asking for a better price after an offer has been accepted. That's not the time for second thoughts. Once an offer is made, you must abide by it. When the offer leaves your lips, it cannot be recalled.

If neither buyer nor seller agrees on the prices offered, the war of nerves begins. This is the time to not be in a hurry. Now the buyer points out the object's faults while the seller tries to convince the buyer that it's impossible to pass up such a deal. Counter offers are made during this time. One ploy used by the buyer is to point out his lack of "money" (rather than the expense of the product). The seller may throw in another object to make the bargain a better deal or remove something from a group of objects being sold to lower the price he's asking.

This goes on until a deal is struck or neither side feels that something can be worked out and the bargaining is halted in a friendly way. Usually, the would-be buyer must stop it. One easy way is to ask for some time to "think about the deal" which is a legitimate request. The seller can offer to remove the object to a back room if the would-be buyer is really interested in buying at a later date. If the buyer isn't interested or isn't sure, then he should allow the seller to place it back out for trade after a certain period of time has passed.

If you run into a person who is hard to bargain with, it often pays to throw him off balance from time to time. Offer him outrageously bad offers, drop something (of yours) and break it, or the like. Jangle the nerves or make him relieved after it's over and you've left. When the dentist looks into your mouth and mutters "Oh, oh," just think how happy you are to only pay a few hundred — rather than thousands — for his work. Use the same type of psychological warfare on the hard-to-trade-with customer.

There are other "tricks" of "psychological warfare" used by businessmen which may be adapted to barter. One is the last-one gambit. It's simple. Let the customer think that the last one of what you have to barter is up for grabs. If he doesn't get it soon on your terms, he'll probably not get it at all. Just don't be too quick to get out your next one of a hundred "last ones" before he leaves your area. It's best to display only one item and let your customer jump to his own conclusions. This makes it possible to mention that you have another one or two in the back room, if he'd like another — just after you've finalized the deal. Usually, you'll have to sense out the customer and adapt to your environment. People who want another of what you're selling will probably give you cues that they'd like another one if you are sensitive enough to read their signals.

Sometimes a second deal can be struck up if you and your would-be barterer can't come to an agreement. This is the time you bring out your damaged or shop-worn duplicate of what he's interested in. This allows you to make a trade, get rid of a somewhat abused piece of merchandise, and still get ahead for the time spent in bargaining.

When you just can't work something out, threaten to quit and forget the whole thing. With many people, this is their cue to make their best offer. If you can operate from a position of "I can live without it" they may be forced to make an offer more to your liking. Again, you'll have to be sensitive to the person you're dealing with and develop good timing with your "take-it-or-leave-it."

Once in a while, a good sob story can be used to create a more favorable deal. Children or spouse sick? Essential machinery broken down? Use your tale of woe to get a little sympathy if it doesn't make you feel too guilty. Just save it for the really desperate time of need and don't abuse it. If you make up a problem every time you meet to barter, word soon gets around.

Always have a good deal or one choice item held in reserve to throw in to finalize the deal. You may not need it but if you do, it's good to be able to pull all your barter power into play for a final chance for what you're trying to get. Your final offer will finish or cut off your bartering most of the time. Sometimes you may also ask the other person to throw in an item or give you something "to boot." This is often a good maneuver to carry out at the last minute to pick up an extra little bit of trade with the next person you encounter in your bartering. "Throw-in four ___'s to boot and you've got a deal" often gives you just a little extra to barter with next time.

Many successful barterers never accept "no" for an answer. They just make another offer until they finally hit upon the right combination and get their trades. This doesn't work for most people, though. Know when to quit; just don't quit too soon!

Some people kill time by striking up a barter situation which they don't expect to follow through on. They carry out the preliminary steps but make such poor, unbending offers that no one can trade with them without coming out short on patience and goods. If you are dealing with someone like this, threaten to stop bargaining if they can't make a reasonable offer. If they don't change their offer, stop bargaining with them.

Another problem is the guy who wants to think about it, and think some more and continues to stall, unable to make up his mind. Your tactic should be to add a time deadline when dealing with this type of person. If you can find someone else who wants the item, add a little competition to your dealings and threaten to make a deal with a third party if your slow trader can't make a decision by a certain time (you might even want to create an imaginary customer). One last ditch method might be to throw in a little extra if he hurries up, though this may cause him to stall next time he's bartering with you in the hope of getting a better deal.

Anything they can do, you can do. So, you might want to follow the reverse of the above and stall a little yourself. When the other trader gets in a hurry, make a lower offer... he may take it or go through the above countermaneuvers. Just don't try this with the guy who wants to think about it or you'll have a never ending trade going.

Try to know as much about what you're trading and what you're trading for as possible. If you don't know the worth of something, chances are you'll come out behind in your trading unless the person trading with you is as ignorant as you are — and then your chances are only 50/50. Sometimes you can protect yourself slightly by telling the person trading with you that the object has sentimental value and that you won't take less than a certain thing or amount for it. This object must be capable of having sentimental worth, of course, and this is also pretty well limits the perimeters of your trading by setting up a limit to what you'll accept. It's best to know as much as possible about the value of what you have.

When finalizing a trade, you may need to make some sort of agreement or document for large barters. This will make sure that both sides understand the terms and have reached the same agreement of terms. Try to make things as simple as possible, don't take anything for granted, and agree to what will happen if one or the other of you doesn't follow through on the terms of your barter. Though contracts may not be enforceable in a barter system because of the lack of government officials and courts, a contract will help to delineate the scope of the deal and may enable you to take steps to straighten things out later without looking like a criminal to those in your community. Even though there is no law enforcement, be sure that your word is as good as any law and keep all verbal and written agreements. This will help you as you continue to barter as people will trust your deals and may even seek you out so that they can deal with a barterer they can trust. Good, truthful practices will help you in the long run.

LIVING IN A BARTER COMMUNITY

Now is the time to prepare for living in a barter community. If you start preparing now, you can pick and choose and be way ahead of most of our society when an economic/monetary collapse results. This head start will enable you to increase your standard of living or wealth without hurting those who are around you. In fact, you will probably help friends and neighbors as well since you will be easing the changeover from cash to barter. In extreme cases, you may even enable many to survive who might perish if you hadn't been preparing.

At the same time, you should be able to come out even — and probably ahead — if things don't go down the tubes and society straightens itself out from the course it seems to be on. No need to sell good clothes for sackcloth and ashes!

One way to prepare is by stockpiling goods which are now cheap and common but which might become scarce during an economic breakdown because they are hard to produce, take special machinery to produce, or must be transported into your area from a distant place. By stockpiling now, you can take advantage of prices when goods are available. You should not feel guilty about stockpiling while goods are plentiful: you will help the present economy and many workers by creating a slightly bigger market for their goods. You will also help out if there is a disaster since you won't be among those who will be out in a panic spree of buying — and looting — to get essential supplies.

Stockpiling allows you to later barter your goods for other needs and can give you a take-it-or-leave-it outlook as you can get by without having to barter with an unfair trader. Not having stockpiled goods to fall back upon — especially during the first few weeks following a disaster — would mean that you and your family would be at the mercy of any selfish, crooked trader with essential goods. The more people who have stockpiled goods, the smaller this crooked trader's market and the less ability he will have to hold numbers of people over a barrel. You may even be able to undercut his "bargains" to keep his prices fair by trading your goods that you've stockpiled. The crooked trader will soon be in disgrace after your community gets back on its feet. Don't be tempted to join his quick-profit-from-disaster technique. He'll probably leave town in a hurry when your area collects its senses.

It is wise to stockpile items which don't presently have great value or which are hard to transport. This will keep you from having trouble with break-ins and the loss of goods because of thievery. What thief is going to carry off 40 pounds of salt or 20 gallons of honey? Yet these things could be essential to you if they aren't produced locally. Once things break down and the stockpiled goods become valuable because of scarcity on the local level, then you can stay home and guard them from thieves (who may soon be a vanishing breed as small barter groups/villages keep track of who has and produces what).

Items which you may wish to consider for stockpiling (provided they aren't produced locally in your area and can be used by you or your family): food, honey, soap and detergents, vitamins and minerals, salt, sugar, knives, hatchets, tools, pens, pencils, needles, and ammunition. Also, consider chemicals, solder, or special metals/tools you might find of use. Most of the items you'll stockpile will have a long or indefinite shelf life provided they are stored in a cool, dry area. The food and ammunition are the only exceptions. Food shelf life varies (rotate your food stockpile...eat what you can no longer store) and the ammunition has a life upward to 20 years if kept cool and dry. Try to stockpile items which could be used by your family even if you are never in a barter situation and which would be easily used by those with whom you would be bartering if you ever do need to barter. With ammunition, for example, you'd be wise to get ammunition of a caliber that is very common rather than something which demands a not too popular weapon to fire it.

When stockpiling, you should also try to diversify when picking out the items you may later be bartering. The cliche of not putting all your eggs in one basket is good to remember. The guy down the block might be storing a ton of .22 ammunition for bartering along with 8 bags of silver coins. The value of goods is often decided by how plentiful they are and if you and your neighbor have both been storing .22 shells and silver, you'll have a pretty poor market when things go to barter. Diversify.

Learning to do many odds and ends yourself, rather than having to ask a specialist to do them for you, can also enable you to keep things going and in effect, increase your wealth. What you would have had to trade for someone's help can be traded for luxuries.

Having only goods to trade is not too good a way to get ahead in increasing your standard of living. In fact, since you have to eat part of what you've saved or bartered goods for, you'll gradually become poorer and poorer unless you can add to what you have. Producing more than you need will enable you to become wealthier as you barter your surplus. Trading only what you already have means your supplies will gradually diminish as you use some of them yourself.

So, you'd also be wise to invest in tools and in learning how to do things now so that you can be self-sufficient and produce more on your own if a barter society develops. Tools can be essential for getting things done. They are also often created by complex industrial processes which aren't rare now, but might be after an economic collapse. How many people in your area can create or build the tools you may need? Even a hammer is almost impossible to make without complex equipment. Buy mass-produced, cheap tools now before all you can get is a second-hand or hand-produced—expensive—model after the economy shrinks. Without the right tools, many simple tasks are all but impossible. Ever try to pound a nail without a hammer or drive a screw without a screwdriver? It's possible but not too practical.

Having a book of formulas or developing a special skill might be like striking gold in your basement. Now is the time to buy cheap reference books and learn how to use them to guide you in doing those simple things which none of us know how to do. If your community is cut off from the outside world, how much can be made and repaired in your area by those you know? Either your group does it or it's not done in such a case.

When tool shopping, avoid power tools unless you plan on generating your own power. Also, be prepared for the idea of switching your car over to alcohol or methane gas. Give some thought as to what you need if national and large power/fuel companies are suddenly no longer able to operate because money has become a thing of the past. Utilities will bog down in the paperwork of barter if not from the lack of fuel. Be ready to do without or do it on your own. What kind of shape would you be in if the community's gas, electricity, water, and sewage systems were shut off for good tonight? Could you get by?

Power tools aren't really needed for most small jobs. Mostly, they are used because they save time and effort. It is also possible to use power other than electricity to run power tools. Wind and water are the most common alternatives. Most small jobs can be done just as well with hand-powered tools though it may take longer and require more physical effort to get the job done.

After an old form of money passes away, it is often replaced by a form of barter money. The new "coinage" must be hard to produce yet plentiful enough to make trade easy. Further, it must be of unvarying quality so that everyone knows its worth and small so that it doesn't require being broken apart to create fractional "change." If you can produce such money, you are in a position of advantage if you can produce it at a cheaper cost to you in time and supplies than it will bring in trade. This is rather tricky to pull off but worth thinking about. If you take the lead in producing such a "coin of the realm" immediately following a crisis when things are just being sorted out, you might corner the "money" market! Ammo, eggs, candy or "?" are all possibilities.

You might also be able to create the barter money after some small item has established itself as the new currency. Be sure your coinage is as good as the accepted type. Making money is "legal" (provided the government doesn't step in and make it illegal for anyone but itself — monopoly at its finest) if it can't be distinguished from the current money and is of the same quality. If you can do all this, and still realize a profit, you are on the path of Midas.

PROTECTING YOURSELF AGAINST CRIMINALS

Whether you deal on the black market (because the government's money is worthless) or an open barter economy (because the government is nonexistent), there will be little or no law enforcement officals to protect you. Hiring someone is expensive. That leaves you to protect yourself. Please note that the law may still exist but there are no law enforcers. Though you control the law enforcers or are enforcing it yourself, you still may be perceived as breaking the law if you take advantage of any strength you have over those who don't have your brawn — hired or otherwise. When your area sorts itself out after the economy has failed, those who are lawless may have to leave town or may even be in "grave" danger. Even if there is no one to force you to obey the law, you must strive to do so while you force others to do so with your might.

That being said, what do you need to protect yourself from any criminals who may try to "muscle-in" in your area?

The answer is probably guns. That may offend many, and most of us would prefer a less lethal solution, but there doesn't seem to be one. Currently, nothing is able to knock out an attacker from the same range and with the same speed as the gun he may be carrying. If criminals played by the rules and could be trusted to not carry and use guns, then another route would be open. They don't and can't; there isn't.

Don't fool yourself about guns. They are made to be lethal and they are. Even the .22 — the smallest caliber readily available — is usually lethal with head and body wounds. That being said, don't buy the smallest caliber weapon believing it to be non-lethal. There is no such gun. There are only different levels of deadliness; no gun is capable of only wounding even 80% of the time.

So, get a caliber that is big enough to protect you. What? Don't all guns kill? So, why not get the small, cheap, small caliber guns? The sad truth is that the small guns kill, but not too quickly, and when they only wound, they don't stop an attacker. The larger guns kill too, but knock your attacker out of action right away most the time. Your best bet is a shotgun. These are awkward to carry, though, so you'll probably want a handgun, too. The caliber recommended is the .45 with the 9mm a runner-up. Get an automatic handgun and practice with it so you will know how to use it and how it works. Hollow point bullets are the most effective and are less apt to richochet if you miss your target. Hollow points are also less apt to travel through whatever you are shooting and hit an innocent person behind your target.

Don't get a gun if you don't think you can use it. If you have a gun, you will probably be killed when robbed rather than just being beaten up as you might be if you didn't have a gun. You should remember that you won't have insurance, welfare, or government breaks if you are robbed. A thief who steals from you may ruin your business and may condemn you to a life of poverty, or even starvation in an extreme instance. Think hard and long about the need to protect yourself, your family, and your business.

If you carry a gun, part of its value is in deterrance. Wear it openly and you may avoid having to use it. Hide it and the criminal may try to rob you. Yes, he'll be surprised but you will risk a lot of trouble, death, and violence if you have to repel his crime because you looked like an easy mark. Unless you have a Clint Eastwood complex, wear your gun openly and hope it deters would-be criminals. A few armed men, who agree to counterattack any robber in a community's bartering area would place the area under an umbrella of protection which would encourage trade and help the community. If you don't wear a gun for personal reasons, then you should support any who help your bartering group by arming themselves. A few "gifts" for their services would probably be in order.

Some people suffer from a need to play Robin Hood. Since there probably won't be any king's men in your area, don't dress up like a rich man. Currently, the rich man who dresses in regular or even too-used clothing and drives a rusted-out car is less apt to be kidnapped or robbed than the guy who acts rich. The same will be especially true when law officers aren't in abundance. Don't invite trouble by excessive displays of wealth. Don't brag about what all you have when you're out in public. Enjoy your high standard of living (or relatively high) in the privacy of your own home — and avoid trouble.

Likewise, don't display all your wares when it's time to carry on public barter. Besides making your barter items appear to be worth less (apparently plentiful supplies on your table seem to mean less demand and therefore less value), it again conveys the feeling that you have more than you need and therefore are a prime target to be Robin Hooded. Don't invite robbery because of your overabundant life style.

When bartering skill, be honest about what you are capable of doing. It's better to understate your ability a little — and let others sing your praises — than to overstate and hear others' curses. Sell yourself but don't lie. You should be trading your skills for an equal value of something else. If you receive more than you are worth, it is the same as the person who trades a defective article when you believe it to be of value.

No matter what the fairy tales may tell you, opportunity probably won't come knocking at your door. You have to go out and grab her by the neck. Even then, it's an uphill struggle to force her to help you out.

When you're bartering, you must think of all the lessons you have received from Madison Avenue in the way of advertising know-how. Sort out the trash and hype and use the professional advertiser's ideas to sell what you have. The guy you're bartering with isn't going to give away his item, and you are the only one who'll get enthused about what you have. Point out its good points and don't be afraid to "sell" your product.

Try to get quick barter deals, and even impulse deals, when trading. The person who needs to think about the deal for a day or two probably won't be bartering with you. Tricks that help to get a quick trade are straight from your local merchant: "Today is the last day it's available, the last product, hurry, limited offer, prices go up tommorrow, it's promised to someone else but..."

Now's the time to practice and hone your skills. Many areas have second-hand stores and flea markets where the people will barter or at least let you haggle about the price in (still accepted) governmental money. Any skill you gain now in bartering will pay big dividends if you are ever forced to engage in an everyday barter economy. Practice until you've learned the tricks that work for you and gained the style that will give you a bartering edge over the average guy.

WHAT YOU CAN BARTER

I can't begin to give all the possibilities that you might think about in the way of things or skills that can be bartered. Time changes people's needs. Services and objects we take for granted may be in short supply some day soon.

At the same time, you can plan on people needing necessities before they demand luxuries. Arts and entertainment can't survive until everyone (or at least the ruler) has a full stomach, isn't worrying about his enemies appearing at the gate, and has time on his hands. At the same time, many who have what might seem to be nonessential talents can develop a necessary skill by adapting to things as they are. Thus, in the past, an artist worked for the church to illustrate stories for the church fathers and the musician told the local news in song and helped everyone forget how bad things were. Not that these methods will work in your area... but get the idea?

Likewise, there are some things which, though needed, aren't needed in sufficient quantity to support the producer unless he branches out beyond the local area. This means he will have to hire — or become — a peddler or traveling salesman.

Specializing can be a double-sided problem. You may beat out all competition if you are skilled enough but you may also find your services aren't needed often enough to pay your bills. You may suddenly be out of business when someone else offers your services at cut rates. Thus, you would be wise to have another way of earning your livelihood to which you can turn if business goes sour.

Get the special tools you need to carry out any skills you have. Get quality tools that will last — you may be passing them down to your son or favorite helper. You should also learn how to make or repair your tools and perhaps even have spare parts to extend the life of complex tools. Don't be afraid to buy a disabled machine or two now to cannibalize parts from, if such a thing is practical (this could also be done after a disaster if worn-out tools are available to cannibalize parts from — one good tool from two ruined ones). Know how your tools work and try to find out which parts will wear out first so you can have spare parts.

Try to take care of any specialized clothing you may need for your job. Reinforce clothing where possible, and change into everyday grubby clothing when possible. Many clothes may be unavailable for some time once you wear out the ones you have.

You may have a skill which has time consuming tasks which don't take much talent to do... or you may have a son or daughter who would like to start working at a craft or profession to make a living... or you may have more customers than you can handle... Apprenticeship is the answer to your needs.

The apprentice does the "dirty work" for free in exchange for being taught a skill by a known artist, craftsman, or other "master." Usually a contract of some sort should be created so the apprentice knows what skill will be taught in exchange for how many years of work. Go into the length of the day's work, who pays for tools, etc., who furnishes room and board. Have an "out" clause so each party knows what happens if one end of the deal isn't held up. Though this need not be in writing, it would probably be a good idea to put it in a permanent form, as such contracts become hazy to the memory after years pass.

If an apprentice travels from place to place "doing his thing" and bringing back the proceeds of his work to his master, he is known as a journeyman. A journeyman increases his master's business and can also create contacts for his own business once he is on his own. He also has a unique chance to scout out surrounding areas so that he will know which area can support him when his apprenticeship ends and he is on his own.

A necessary part of apprenticeship is to learn how to make the tools of the trade. Once the apprentice has learned this and has created his tools, he is on his way toward making his living.

The apprentice need not become a competitor. If both apprentice and master are talented and get along together, they can become partners. One has new ideas and energy to add to the business and the other a ready clientele and an established business with all the tools, place of business, and stock ready to go.

Peddlers are people who travel from place to place bartering some service or small portable necessities for what they need to make a living. Peddlers have the advantage of being able to travel from place to place... also, the disadvantage of having to travel from place to place. If you choose this style of living, be sure to learn how to make "traveling light" work to your advantage.

Like other forms of barter, the peddler must either barter goods or his skills. In the interest of traveling easily, and quickly if necessary, skills are the best ware to barter. Goods are great if they are mobile or if you have a method of moving them (or if they are self-propelled as in the case of animals).

If you peddle goods, you'll have to learn how to be a good horse trader and how to work trades to your advantage. As other people become used to bartering, you will have a harder time getting the best deals.

As a peddler, you'll have to be sharp enough to avoid irate bargainers, feuds, fights, and be able to keep from wandering into the hands of robbers. Additionally, most areas you go into would probably be sorely lacking in law enforcement.

All in all, being a peddler would probably not be very wise or safe. It would be an adventurous endeavor.

I will now discuss skills, crafts, and services. They serve to spark the imagination of those who don't possess barterable skills or who wish to cover another area to fall back on in severe conditions.

Some skills will be needed which have become almost nonexistent in our industrialized society. Here's a list of those: tailor, cobbler, weaver, tinkerer, fix-it-man, grinder/sharpener, paper maker, printer, and carpenter. Most of these skills are easily learned but require a lot of practice before any finesse is acquired.

Hunting and trapping may furnish much of the meat and furs in your area, but chances are some sort of farming will have to be carried out to supply a community's needs. Many techniques which are almost forgotten by most farmers will have to be revived and used on the farm. The farm will be producing *and* processing much of the food and possibly the leather and furs for the area.

Methods of storing and processing foods as well as curing meats and tanning hides are covered in the books in the Bibliography. Using the methods outlined in these books, you can store and process food without using electricity or modern refrigeration methods, a plus you may find very useful.

If you learn to butcher, harvest, etc., you may find that you can trade your skill for part of a final product. Likewise, if you have land for animals, you may be able to trade its use in logging, trapping, mowing (for hay), or the grazing of animals in exchange for a percentage of the product.

Eggs are a product you should consider (whether you plan to farm on a full scale or only produce enough food for your family's needs). The only bad thing about eggs is that you need chickens, or another egg laying domesticated bird, to obtain them. Chickens are dirty, dumb animals that will eat anything including each other. After you've been around them a while, you'll learn to look down upon them with a righteous superiority complex; but their eggs are unbelievable in their storage life and nutritional value.

To store eggs, place them in a cool, dry area where they will not freeze, with the small end of the egg pointed down. For long term storage, brush gum arabic on the shells and store in a cool, dry area with the eggs packed in charcoal dust. If you really want to go all out, eggs can be stored up to two years by placing them under water which has the following mixture added to it: 1 bushel of quicklime, 2 pounds of salt, and 1/2 pound of cream of tarter (you may wish to reduce this according to how many eggs you have). The amount of water is determined by adding just enough to allow only the top of the egg to float above water. When all the eggs are placed in the mixture, a cover is placed on the container to force the top eggs below the water line.

Cats might be very useful animals to have around your area. Feed them enough to encourage them to stay around but still be happy to hunt down rats and mice on their own. A cat can keep the rodent population down and prevent disease and food damage to your household. If you are blessed with a female cat, you'll probably soon have some cats to barter.

When picking plants to grow, try to select non-hybrid plants as they will produce seeds which can be used to grow new plants for another season. Learn how to go about pruning fruit trees and how to use natural fertilizers and how to make-do without insecticides if they aren't available.

Ideally, no one would ever get sick; but you can bet that sooner or later, you or someone in your family will need some medical help. Since there will probably be no state health officials or medical "watch dogs" to protect the public, you must be sure that anyone who is offering his services to you isn't a quack. Know where a good doctor, dentist, midwife, or druggist is before you need such a person.

It might also be wise to know something about what is going on with any human bodies under your charge. Learn some first-aid and know what to do for common "emergencies." There are many books available that will help you in your learning. Just don't get overly confident and try to do more than you can handle. Surgery and much medication is best left to the experts; sometimes doing nothing is better than doing the wrong thing. The human body can often take care of itself if you allow it to.

Several medical books which you might find of use are listed in the Bibliography.

Chances are good that your sight will change as you grow older. Though used/old spectacles probably won't be exactly right for your eyes, they might be an improvement. If an optician isn't in your neighborhood, you might be able to help yourself by experimenting with any old lenses that are available. Far sightedness caused by age is cured by magnifying glasses (convex lens) and near sightedness — which is harder to correct — with a reducing lens (concave lens). It would also be wise to have spare glasses, if you need them, so that an accidental breakage doesn't send you on a quest for the elusive lens that is yours alone.

Local government may start up in your area. Its form will probably be strange at best. If groups are bartering protection, you would be wise to watch that they don't decide to become feudal lords and live it up on others' hard work. The more people you have taking turns at furnishing security patrols and the like, the less apt you are to have a self-chosen few try to take control of your area.

Transporting messages, mail, or people could be a possiblility if you have a vehicle, horse, or lots of foot-powered help.

If you have special machinery or animals which can be used to plow or do special tasks (a chainsaw for example) you can barter the use of them for specific goods or a part of the end product. If you have a lot tied up in the machinery or aren't too sure about the care it will get in the hands of someone else, you might want to do the work yourself or let a trusted apprentice handle the work.

If your local utility service goes off the line for good, your area will have a huge demand for lighting and energy producing equipment. Skills like candle making (and bee keeping for the wax) and creating fat or oil from plants and animals which can be burned in lamps would probably do well. Being able to create methane generators, switch cars and trucks over to methane gas, and being able to build fireplaces and/or steam engines would make you very popular in the barter community.

Information can mean a higher standard of living for your community group. If your area has a public library, guard it like Fort Knox. If you allow volumes to disappear, they will be worth much less than if they are in the library where they can be located quickly when needed and where they are tied into the card catalog. Being able to go to an encyclopedia to find the techniques involved in a skill or in building a forgotten type of machine would save years or even decades of experimenting. Your community may even be able to barter its brainpower/library research abilities with other communities for supplies and services.

Craftsmen such as potters, blacksmiths, and even needle and pin makers will be more and more in demand as many items wear out or are lost.

If guns become necessary to keep things in order in your area, or even to defend your community group from outside force, then a local gunsmith will be needed. The gunsmith needs special screwdrivers, files, vises, metal and wood working tools and, most of all, books which tell how to go about his task. Given the time and know-how, most tools can be built for gunsmithing from scratch and most of the replacement parts for the guns he will be working on can be made from scrap parts.

The community and the gunsmith should encourage everyone to obtain and use guns in the more common calibers. This will make reloading, repair, etc., easier and cheaper for all involved.

The gunsmith should allow trade-ins whenever possible. This takes used and worn-out guns off the market, gives him a gun to repair and resell, and keeps him from losing a sale since he'll have the old gun rather than a potential customer. The same goes for fired shells. If the gunsmith can get the spent cases for reloading, he corners that market.

Modern reloading of shells makes use of ready-made primers and powder. These can be "home-brewed," however, if you know the technique. Some books in the Bibliography outline much of this information which would allow you to manufacture your own powder and recharge the primers for your shells.

Whether you plan on doing gunsmith work or just hope to keep your weapons going, the Lee Loader is a tool which is small enough to carry but which works well when it's needed. Full length sizing is needed if the shell will be used in a gun other than the one it was fired in. If shells will be fired from the same gun, all that needs to be resized is the neck of the shell on most tapered rifle shells. The Lee Loader would also be useful for the gunsmith who did not wish to invest a lot of money in dies for working with off-beat calibers of shells. In such a case, he could buy some Lee Loaders in the seldom used calibers and be able to reload the rare calibers without investing a lot in the tools. Lee Loaders are available from many mail-order firms.

Some books which would be of use to you if you're interested in gunsmithing work are listed in the Bibliography. After you get through these, you'll probably be able to decide whether you want more books or whether you're getting in over your head. Once you've decided, then you should either try to build up your library with more book knowledge or try to locate someone who can do gunsmith work for you.

Your local news service will probably be crude. You may not even need one. A one page gossip sheet, a town crier/watchman, or a traveling troubadour are all likely possibilities. Shortwave or CB radio might also bring you news information from outside your area. Chances are, word of mouth and traveling salesmen along with the radio broadcast will satisfy the news needs of your community.

Luxury items like perfume, cosmetics, etc., will probably have to be made by the individuals who use them. Could you supply your family?

A barter culture will probably not be blessed with TV or cheap entertainment. This probably means that people will have to entertain themselves with reading, games, and amatuer muscial/drama performances.

The possibility of traveling entertainers like jugglers, acrobats, musicians, actors, and the like does exist, but seems very unlikely at least for the first few years as a barter society establishes itself. If such professions do develop, the artists will have to learn how to travel light and how to cater to the public rather than trying to satisfy any artistic or intellectual expressions they may feel the need to share.

Hopefully, by now you've picked up a lot of ideas and have some feeling as to what type of skills you might be able to coax and develop. Too, you should have some new ideas which were sparked by reading this book.

Your next step is to gather the odds and ends you need to be as self-sufficient as you can be and to carry out the profession or production you plan on bartering.

After this, you should practice and develop your skills both in bartering and in what you hope to produce to barter. Only practice will take the rough edges off and hone your skills to their sharpest edge.

Now, it's up to you.

RECOMMENDED READING

*Readers of **Survival Bartering** will also find the following books and sources useful.*

The Alpha Strategy, by John A. Pugsley. An excellent book on stockpiling and hoarding, and how you can profit from doing so, even if an emergency never occurs. Available from Loompanics Unlimited, PO Box 1197, Port Townsend, WA 98368.

American Survival Guide, McMullen Publishing Inc., 2145 W. La Palma Ave., Anaheim, CA 92801. Excellent monthly magazine covering all aspects of survival and self-sufficiency. Great ads, too.

Atlan Formularies, PO Box 327, Harrison, AR 72601. Publisher and seller of survival books, such as ***Grandad's Wonderful Book Of Chemistry,*** etc.

The Barter Book, by Dyanne Asimow Simon. One of the best barter books. Very sympathetic with the "underground" possibilities inherent in bartering. Out of print — look for it in a library.

Brigade Quartermaster, 226 Roswell St., Marietta, GA 30060. Sellers of army surplus and survival gear.

Checklist For Survival, by Tony & Jo-Anne Lesce. A good book on what to stock up on to prepare for emergencies. Paladin Press, PO Box 1307, Boulder, CO 80306.

Crisis Preparedness Handbook, by Jack A. Spigarelli. Excellent and comprehensive guide to home storage and physical survival. Resource Publications, PO Box 1515, Provo, UT 84603.

Emergency War Surgery, by the US Department of Defense. Available from US Government Printing Office, Superintendent of Documents, Washington, DC 20402. For when the going gets really tough.

Firearms Assembly/Disassembly. Multiple volumes by L.B. Wood. DBI Books, One Northfield Plaza, Northfield, IL 60093. This company also has good books on reloading.

Garden Way Books/Storey Communications, Inc., Schoolhouse Road, Pownal, VT 05261. Publishers of an excellent series of homestead books covering raising and storing food, alternate energy, tanning hides, keeping bees, and much more.

Guerrilla Capitalism, by Adam Cash. A how-to-do-it book on the underground economy. Very useful. 1984, Loompanics Unlimited, PO Box 1197, Port Townsend, WA 98368.

Henley's Twentieth Century Book Of Ten Thousand Recipes, Formulas And Processes. The "Bible" of home production. How to make everything from toothpaste to varnish. Available from Loompanics Unlimited, PO Box 1197, Port Townsend, WA 98368.

Homemade Guns and Homemade Ammo, by Ronald B. Brown. Excellent book on making guns and ammunition from simple materials. Loompanics Unlimited, PO Box 1197, Port Townsend, WA 98368.

How To Hide Anything, by Michael Connor. Very useful book on concealing whatever you have to hide. Paladin Press, PO Box 1307, Boulder, CO 80306.

Let's Try Barter, by Charles Morrow Wilson. Now out of print, but a good book on general bartering — look for it in a library.

The Merck Manual. Professional medical manual, should be in everyone's survival/self-sufficiency kit. Merck Sharp and Dohme Research Laboratories, Rahway, NJ.

Mother Earth News, Box 70, Hendersonville, NC 28791. Periodical for homesteaders and back-to-the-landers — very useful. They also operate a book service.

Pistol-Smithing, George C. Nonte, Jr. Stackpole Books, Cameron and Kelker Streets, Harrisburg, PA 17105. This company also has other good books on gunsmithing.

The Ship's Medicine Chest. HEW Publication No. (HSA) 78-2024 from the US Government Printing Office, Superintendent of Documents, Washington, DC 20402.

The Survival Retreat, by Ragnar Benson. Very practical and down-to-earth book on putting together a safe place. Paladin Press, PO Box 1307, Boulder, CO 80306.

Survivalist's Medicine Chest, by Ragnar Benson. How to stockpile medicines, with emphasis on buying them cheap. Paladin Press, PO Box 1307, Boulder, CO 80306.

CONTROVERSIAL AND UNUSUAL BOOKS!!!

"Yes, there are books about the skills of apocalypse -- spying, surveillance, fraud, wire-tapping, smuggling, self-defense, lockpicking, gunmanship, eavesdropping, car chasing, civil warfare, surviving jail, and dropping out of sight. Apparently writing books is the way mercenaries bring in spare cash between wars. The books are useful, and it's good the information is freely available (and they definitely inspire interesting dreams), but their advice should be taken with a salt shaker or two and all your wits. A few of these volumes are truly scary. Loompanics is the best of the Libertarian suppliers who carry them. Though full of 'you'll-wish-you'd-read-these-when-it's-too-late' rhetoric, their catalog is genuinely informative."

-THE NEXT WHOLE EARTH CATALOG

Now available:
THE BEST BOOK CATALOG IN THE WORLD!!!

- *Large 8½ x 11 size!*
- *More than 500 of the most controversial and unusual books ever printed!!!*
- *YOU can order EVERY book listed!!!*
- *Periodic Supplements to keep you posted on the LATEST titles available!!!*

We offer hard-to-find books on the world's most unusual subjects. Here are a few of the topics covered IN DEPTH in our exciting new catalog:

- *Hiding/concealment of physical objects! A complete section of the best books ever written on hiding things!*
- *Fake ID/Alternate Identities! The most comprehensive selection of books on this little-known subject ever offered for sale! You have to see it to believe it!*
- *Investigative/Undercover methods and techniques! Professional secrets known only to a few, now revealed for YOU to use! Actual police manuals on shadowing and surveillance!*
- *And much, much more, including Locks and Locksmithing, Self Defense, Intelligence Increase, Life Extension, Money-Making Opportunities, and much, much more!*

Our book catalog is truly THE BEST BOOK CATALOG IN THE WORLD! Order yours today -- you will be very pleased, we know.

(Our catalog is free with the order of any book on the previous page -- or is $2.00 if ordered by itself.)

Loompanics Unlimited
PO Box 1197
Pt Townsend, WA 98368
USA